Dwell

WONDER

An Advent Devotional

Published by Dwell

Cover design by Justin Skinner

Interior design by Andy Meaden / meadencreative.com

Contents

Introduction

"The world will never starve for want of wonders, but only for want of wonder."

-G.K. CHESTERTON

When was the last time you were overcome by wonder? Not simple curiosity, admiration, or even respect, but awe-inspiring, ground-shaking, undeniable wonder. A first kiss or a child's first breath. The ocean at sunset or a mountain's peak at sunrise. A symphony orchestra or a medieval cathedral.

Wonder draws us out of ourselves and into that which is beyond comprehension or explanation. It reframes and reshapes the realities of our lives, refusing to leave us the same as we once were. It may only last a moment, yet its impact on our lives cannot be overstated.

The birth of Christ is the wonder of wonders, yet does it awaken in you a deep and abiding sense of wonder? Put another way, do you enter into the Advent season with a sense of awe and anticipation at the reality and mystery of God drawing near in Christ? Or, is your wonder lost in a familiar wave of nostalgia, consumerism, anxiety, and stress?

We must learn to cultivate a life of wonder.

We choose to gaze at stars and into a lover's eyes, and we choose to open our hearts to the reality of the Incarnation. This entry into a life of wonder invites daily attentiveness and intentionality. We say no to the distractions and habits that numb our senses and callous our souls, contenting us with lesser loves and disposable joys.

In this collection of daily readings for Advent, you are invited into a life of wonder. As you reflect upon Scripture and seek to apply it to your daily life, let it awaken in you a longing and desire for God. Believe that the Spirit will meet and lead you on this journey, tuning your heart to what is truly good, beautiful, and worthy of wonder.

FIRST WEEK *of* ADVENT

SUNDAY

Pray. Look. Listen.

(▶) Open Dwell and listen to the following in the *Wonder* plan:
**Jeremiah 33:14-16 | Psalm 25:1-10 | 1 Thessalonians 3:9-13 |
Luke 21:25-36**

"Sin is a wound. Repentance is a medicine."

-St. John Chrysostom

Advent is fundamentally and unquestionably a story of God's faithfulness to his people in and through the birth of Jesus Christ. It is too glorious a story for us to imagine and more lavishly extravagant than we can begin to fathom. Though Advent is an invitation that invites a response, its arrival is entirely independent of our ability to control or contrive.

In fact, *adventus*, the Latin word from which this great season receives its name, means "arrival." In many ways, this is a lens through which we can read the story of Scripture. The entire Bible is filled with moments of God's arrival, his breaking in to the story of creation and breathing life where there is death, peace where there is chaos, and hope where there is despair. And yet, it seems with each arrival that his presence was so often met with fear, skepticism, or outright disobedience.

Our alienation from God is a self-made isolation. Though he never ceases to pour out his love upon us, we all too easily turn away from this love, failing to see his love that is with us wherever we go. And so, as we begin this season, we are today invited to do three things: Pray. Look. Listen.

We *pray* for the humility and repentance of David, who, though painfully aware of his own shortcomings, pursued the Lord to the very end: *Lead me, teach me, for you I wait all day long* (Ps 25:5). Likewise, *we look back* to the ancient story of old, seeing how God in Christ has fulfilled all of his promises to the house of Israel (Jer 33:14). And lastly, we *listen* to the words of Christ, who not only came as a child but promises to come again in power and glory, inviting us to "be alert at all times" (Luke 21:36), anticipating our Lord's *Second* Advent.

Pray. Look. Listen. This is the heart of Advent, the return of the prodigal, and the way of holiness that prepares us to greet the Lord when he comes with all his saints (1 Thess 3:13).

Prayer for the Week

Almighty God, give us grace to cast away the works of darkness, and put on the armor of light, now in the time of this mortal life in which your Son Jesus Christ came to visit us in great humility; that in the last day, when he shall come again in his glorious majesty to judge both the living and the dead, we may rise to the life immortal; through him who lives and reigns with you and the Holy Spirit, one God, now and for ever. *Amen.*

Reflective Practice

Advent requires preparation and intentionality. From day one, how can you carve out space for a meaningful rhythm of prayer and attentiveness to God over the coming weeks? Take time today to write out and document a few goals for this Advent season.

Notes

_____

_____

_____

_____

_____

_____

_____

_____

_____

MONDAY

Who Are You?

▶ Open Dwell and listen to the following in the *Wonder* plan:
Psalm 90 | Numbers 17:1-11 | 2 Peter 3:1-18

"Do not give your heart to that which does not satisfy your heart."

-ABBA POEMEN

"What sort of people ought you to be?" (2 Pet 3:11). This is the question St. Peter poses to the early church and to us in today's reading. In our digital age, with endless information at our fingertips, the quest for *knowledge* can often overshadow the deeper invitation into transformed *living*. Peter is aware of something that we are quick to forget: knowledge and information, though important, are not the ultimate aims of the Christian life. No, to follow Christ is to become a living embodiment of his coming kingdom.

It is entirely possible to know a great deal about Jesus Christ and yet never know him.

According to Peter, we hasten the coming kingdom of God and eagerly anticipate it as we live "holy and godly lives." This is who we are meant to be and the way of living we resolve to pursue with all our strength. Again, it must be emphasized: this cannot be reduced to simple moralism, people who "do this and not that." Morality is a fruit of an abiding life with Christ, but do not mistake it for life itself.

Lives that are holy are lives that are filled with the fire of God and conformed to his will through daily surrender and repentance. We become like God as we give ourselves away in love and service to our neighbor. There is no other way. And so, in Advent, we learn to wait for our Lord, not in apathy or inattentiveness but in a daily encounter with his Spirit that brings his peace and moves our hearts in wonder and worship.

Prayer for the Week

Almighty God, give us grace to cast away the works of darkness, and put on the armor of light, now in the time of this mortal life in which your Son Jesus Christ came to visit us in great humility; that in the last day, when he shall come again in his glorious majesty to judge both the living and the dead, we may rise to the life immortal; through him who lives and reigns with you and the Holy Spirit, one God, now and for ever. *Amen.*

Reflective Practice

Are there ways in which you have conflated knowledge of God and a living encounter with God? Reflect upon a few areas of Christian knowledge—such as theology, history, or liturgy—and ask whether these have led not simply to an expanded understanding of faith but to an abiding relationship with Christ.

Notes

TUESDAY

Good and True

(▶) Open Dwell and listen to the following in the *Wonder* plan:
Psalm 90 | 2 Samuel 7:18-29 | Revelation 22:12-16

"If you are seeking the place of God, a pure heart is His place."

-ORIGEN

The promises of God are good and true.

A promise that is good, yet made without any intention of keeping it, is no promise at all and, in fact, leaves the recipient of the promise worse off than when they started! The promise of a delicious meal to a hungry child is good, yet if it is not true, if the promise is hollow and empty, the child is left more hungry than they would have been otherwise. Goodness without truth is ultimately cruel and deeply unloving.

2 Samuel 7:28 reminds us that God has promised good and glorious things to his people and has every intention of keeping his promise: "And now, O Lord God, you are God, and your words are true, and you have promised this good thing to your servant." Today, as we read these ancient words, we read them alongside the words of Jesus in Revelation 22:16: "I am the root and the descendant of David, the bright morning star." Jesus, time and time again, is revealed to the world as the consummation of the promise made to the house of Israel.

Prophecy and gospel. Promise and fulfillment. Goodness and truth. With these movements we are brought closer and closer to the heart of Advent. In his birth, Jesus reveals to Israel that God's promises are true, that their cries of "How long, O Lord?" (Ps 13:1) have been heard. And in his life, death, resurrection, and ascension, at every step we see the goodness of God's promises, how in Christ he loves us "to the very end" (John 13:1).

Prayer for the Week

Almighty God, give us grace to cast away the works of darkness, and put on the armor of light, now in the time of this mortal life in which your Son Jesus Christ came to visit us in great humility; that in the last day, when he shall come again in his glorious majesty to judge both the living and the dead, we may rise to the life immortal; through him who lives and reigns with you and the Holy Spirit, one God, now and for ever. *Amen.*

Reflective Practice

How does Advent reframe the promises of God or reorient you to his mercy and goodness? Framed another way, are there ways in which you still struggle to believe God is good and desires good for you? From a place of honesty and vulnerability, confess these to the Lord in prayer.

Notes

WEDNESDAY

Our Dwelling Place

(▶) Open Dwell and listen to the following in the *Wonder* plan:
Psalm 90 | Isaiah 1:24-31 | Luke 11:29-32

"For anyone who dwells in darkness will be in desire for the light, but once he comes into the light, then enjoyment displaces desire."

-St. Macrina the Younger

Advent is at the same time a historic event and a present reality. Neither truth can be dismissed, and the fullness of the season is found in the perpetual embrace of this dual reality. Christ came to specific people in a defined region at a fixed point in history. And yet he continues to come, to arrive, as he is present to his people in every place and every age.

If we only focus on the birth of Christ, Advent becomes nothing more than a historic curiosity of interest to a select few yet easily ignored and dismissed by the masses. At the same time, if Jesus is nothing more than a generalized idea of virtue and morality, without any grounding in his life and teaching, he is easily misconstrued and made to fit an endless list of ever-evolving philosophies. Jesus can be neither relegated to the history books nor conformed to the spirit of the age.

Amidst this tension, the psalmist offers an image that we would be wise to take to heart: "Lord, you have been our dwelling place in all generations" (Ps 90:1). To live and to breathe is to be upheld by the sustaining presence of God. As the psalmist says elsewhere, "Where can I flee from your presence?" (Ps 139:7). It is in him that we "live and move and have our being" (Acts 17:28). This has always been true, as the psalmist celebrates, and yet in Advent we celebrate and marvel at the wonder of God's presence with us: the one in whom we live chooses to live with us.

And so, let us remember and reflect upon the birth of Christ in the manger not as a distant reality but as the abiding reality of God with us, now and forever.

Prayer for the Week

Almighty God, give us grace to cast away the works of darkness, and put on the armor of light, now in the time of this mortal life in which your Son Jesus Christ came to visit us in great humility; that in the last day, when he shall come again in his glorious majesty to judge both the living and the dead, we may rise to the life immortal; through him who lives and reigns with you and the Holy Spirit, one God, now and for ever. *Amen.*

Reflective Practice

What are the various "dwellings" in which you seek to find refuge apart from the sustaining presence of Christ? Take time to name them and allow the nearness of Christ to reframe them and cast them in a different light.

Notes

THURSDAY

What Are We Waiting For?

▶ Open Dwell and listen to the following in the *Wonder* plan:
Luke 1:68-79 | Malachi 3:5-12 | Philippians 1:12-18

"Everything comes from love, all is ordained for the salvation of man, God does nothing without this goal in mind."

-St. Catherine of Siena

Observing Advent may seem, in some ways, as if we're pretending. Jesus has already been born, the Word already made flesh, for about 2,000 years now. Why hold off with the parties? We might feel like children suspending disbelief in order to enjoy a puppet show, or a cat energetically pretending that a paper ball is a mouse. In other words, Advent is a nice tradition and all, but is there spiritual truth in this play? What are we *really* waiting for?

First and foremost, we're waiting with someone. "Advent" means "coming." We're waiting with Jesus, in all his divine and human glory, for his return to us. We're waiting with one another, too, for that same thing.

In a sense, we also wait with Mother Mary, who is an ancient symbol of the Church and forerunner of all those who wait with Christ. By putting ourselves in the suspenseful place of all those waiting for his birth—Joseph, the Magi, the prophets, all of God's ancient people—though they hardly knew what they were waiting for, we better prepare ourselves for our own waiting. We, too, can barely imagine "what God has prepared for those who love him" (1 Cor 2:9).

Malachi and Zechariah express hopes for both of Jesus' advents. The hope is beautiful and serious, joyful and dramatic: that we would be "saved from our enemies and the hand of all who hate us" and saved from all our own tragic and futile ways—not just longing for but actually able to live "in holiness and righteousness" (Luke 1:71, 75). Through Christ, we will not be destroyed; we will also cease to take part in destruction. He comes to make of our hearts, lives, and every human habitation "a land of delight" (Mal 3:12). This is what Jesus' advent means and what we take this time to wait for and remember. This may take imagination, but it is definitely not pretend!

Prayer for the Week

Almighty God, give us grace to cast away the works of darkness, and put on the armor of light, now in the time of this mortal life in which your Son Jesus Christ came to visit us in great humility; that in the last day, when he shall come again in his glorious majesty to judge both the living and the dead, we may rise to the life immortal; through him who lives and reigns with you and the Holy Spirit, one God, now and for ever. *Amen.*

Reflective Practice

God means for all human communities and all the earth to be "a land of delight." He fulfills that promise when Christ comes. Do you believe he is fulfilling it now? In your prayer time today, take a moment to tell God where you struggle to see, or to hope to see, this delightful vision. Ask him to renew the eyes of your heart to not pretend everything is okay or easy in this time of waiting but to increase in the discipline of hope.

Notes

_____

_____

_____

_____

_____

_____

_____

FRIDAY

Revere the Lord

▶ Open Dwell and listen to the following in the *Wonder* plan:
Luke 1:68-79 | Malachi 3:13-18 | Philippians 1:18-26

"When you begin to read or listen to the Holy Scriptures, pray to God thus: 'Lord Jesus Christ, open the ears and eyes of my heart so that I may hear Thy words and understand them, and may fulfill Thy will.' Always pray to God like this, that He might illumine your mind and open to you the power of His words. Many, having trusted in their own reason, have turned away into deception."

-St. Ephrem The Syrian

The word for "to wait" or "to expect" in French is *attendre*, "attend," which is also an older English way to say "listen." Advent waiting includes listening carefully—attending—to the story of Israel: startling intimacies with God, stunning failures, weariness with struggle, and weariness with waiting on God. Which one of us cannot sympathize with this drama?

One important thing we learn about in Malachi is the difference between those who are ready to receive the Lord when he comes and those who are not. To some extent, it's true that those who are not ready for the coming of the Lord's deliverance want it on their own terms. It's fair to say that they want earthly justice, prosperity, and happiness to the neglect of holiness, trust, and desire for God's friendship. "What do we profit by keeping his command?" (Mal 3:14).

But we must go beyond that. It's not wrong to want any of these earthly goods. In fact, it is right. God's promises include all earthly right-ness and happiness. "Without fear, in holiness *and* righteousness" is the way Luke 1:75 describes God's desire for human living. Right-eous-ness is when everything is as it should be, as Jesus' prayer puts it, "on earth as in heaven." Those who are not yet ready to receive God's gifts are those who may desire many of the right things but do not believe *God will really bring them to pass*. However, "those who revere the LORD" (Mal 3:16) don't give up. They consider "his name" (Mal 3:16)—recall God's reputation, rely on his character—and they choose to trust him (multiple times a day). There is still struggle, but they make God a friend. "They shall be mine, says the LORD of hosts" (Mal 3:17).

Of course, the Lord will reveal his plan whether we're ready or not. But if we attend to Israel's family history, we may better understand our hope and be more prepared to receive God's gifts with open hands.

Prayer for the Week

Almighty God, give us grace to cast away the works of darkness, and put on the armor of light, now in the time of this mortal life in which your Son Jesus Christ came to visit us in great humility; that in the last day, when he shall come again in his glorious majesty to judge both the living and the dead, we may rise to the life immortal; through him who lives and reigns with you and the Holy Spirit, one God, now and for ever. *Amen.*

Reflective Practice

What do you have the most trouble waiting for? What makes you the most angry or despairing when you don't receive it quickly, either from God or from others? Prayerfully consider these questions today. You may want to spend 5-10 whole minutes meditating on each question. Consider praying with your hands opened upward, as if letting go. Ask the Lord to show you something about your heart. Ask him to help you loosen your grip and trust him.

Notes

_____

_____

_____

SATURDAY

A Feast of Mercy

(▶) Open Dwell and listen to the following in the *Wonder* plan:
Luke 1:68-79 | Malachi 4:1-6 | Luke 9:1-6

"Where there is charity and wisdom, there is neither fear nor ignorance."

-St. Francis of Assisi

We have a great hope when we believe the Lord's promise—a great hope for ourselves and for our world. And yet, for three more weeks, while we keep the hope in one hand, nurturing it and desiring its fulfillment, we hold in the other hand all that has not yet been fulfilled.

It's like we're characters in the film *Babette's Feast*. We know we're in for a beautiful, sumptuous meal, and though we may have *some* idea of what that means (depending on how well we know the chef), we have no idea, really, what the final spread will look like or how or when it's going to be prepared. Or, for that matter, whether we'll like every dish.

So much about the Messiah's coming will be a surprise. But today, we also get a sneak peek into the kitchen, into God's method of deliverance. Christian tradition has always associated charity—God's perfect, clear-eyed, blazing love—with fire. So, apparently, does the Bible. If God's defeat of evil will be like a blazing fire that leaves nothing of injustice but ashes, God's plan involves helping us not only to stand the heat, to be made pure and holy ourselves, but also to get in the kitchen and work with him, transforming everything that can be transformed—the raw ingredients of a sinful, broken life—by the fire of his love into a feast of his mercy.

Today, we might see Jesus' disciples in the Gospels as sous-chefs, with strict instructions on how to begin their work. But there are two important things: only he can instruct them, and only he can give them power. We wait with longing for that which only the chef can do. In the meantime, unlike the perplexed and dubious dinner guests in *Babette's Feast*, let us come close into the kitchen, close to the heat, and know the chef's ways. When he bids us feast, let us not hold back. Let us also be ready to serve.

Prayer for the Week

Almighty God, give us grace to cast away the works of darkness, and put on the armor of light, now in the time of this mortal life in which your Son Jesus Christ came to visit us in great humility; that in the last day, when he shall come again in his glorious majesty to judge both the living and the dead, we may rise to the life immortal; through him who lives and reigns with you and the Holy Spirit, one God, now and for ever. *Amen.*

Reflective Practice

Choose a time this week to watch *Babette's Feast.* As you watch the film, ask yourself how Babette reflects the ministry of Christ and the invitation of God. Or, if you prefer, as you prepare food this week, ask God to prepare you, transform you, and use your life to nourish others. As you sit down to eat, imagine that the Lord has made this meal for you with his own hands. If you're not in the habit of saying a slow or meaningful grace before meals, try it this Advent season.

Notes

_____

_____

_____

_____

_____

_____

_____

SECOND WEEK *of*

ADVENT

SUNDAY

The Rescue of God

▶ Open Dwell and listen to the following in the *Wonder* plan:
Malachi 3:1-4 | Luke 1:68-79 | Philippians 1:3-11 | Luke 3:1-6

"I prefer death in Christ Jesus to power over the farthest limits of the earth. He who died in place of us is the one object of my quest. He who rose for our sakes is my one desire."

-St. Ignatius of Antioch

If you've ever lived in or near the mountains, you've seen what dynamite, bulldozers, controlled burns, earthmovers, and asphalt can do. It's truly astonishing. What was once an impossible or difficult passage, full of many dangers, becomes a smooth highway. However, there is always a cost to such an achievement. To make these roads, homes, family land, wildlife, and their habitats are always displaced or destroyed to some degree. With enough resources, humans can literally move mountains. But there is always a cost. With all our knowledge, technology, and careful planning, there is still so much we don't know about the ripple effects of applying such force to the earth.

God has a different way. When the "messenger of the covenant" comes, the earth and its people won't know what hit them: "Who can endure the day of his coming, and who can stand when he appears?" (Mal 3:2). Scripture tells us he will come in the full power of God, with fire, modifying the inner and outer landscapes of the world we know. And yet, rather than simply being told that this is God's will and we'd better just cut our losses and get over it, we're told repeatedly that this is our hope—that this, and only this, will save us.

It may sound like destruction, and some things will have to go—arrogant pride and all of Satan's deceptions will crumble—but this is the beginning of the rescue of God, the rescue of all creation. It's not a divine vanity project, ego trip, or even the quickest way between two points. Though amazing, human force always has its victims. God's force always rescues victims. In the most naked revelation of his power, a human being on a cross, God became a victim.

As we wait for the birth of Christ, let us listen, along with God's people, to creation's longing for an earth-shaking salvation, for the road of righteousness to be complete. As we hear in Zechariah's song, in this hope alone will be our everlasting peace.

Prayer for the Week

Merciful God, who sent your messengers the prophets to preach repentance and prepare the way for our salvation: Give us grace to heed their warnings and forsake our sins, that we may greet with joy the coming of Jesus Christ our Redeemer; who lives and reigns with you and the Holy Spirit, one God, now and for ever. *Amen.*

Reflective Practice

While walking, driving, or riding today, take time to notice where God's righteousness and peace have yet to be completed in human and non-human creation. Where do you see signs of human power at odds with God's power? Where do you see hope? Turn these observations to prayer and, perhaps, as the Lord leads, let them become longings that inspire prayer throughout Advent.

Notes

_____

_____

_____

_____

_____

_____

MONDAY

Seeds of Hope

▶ Open Dwell and listen to the following in the *Wonder* plan:
Psalm 126 | Isaiah 40:1-11 | Romans 8:22-25

"It is impossible to draw near to God without sorrows."

-St. Isaac The Syrian

Most of us don't run farms, but many of us have gardens or at least potted plants. Still, how many of us have ever done any planting or sowing while crying? What is there to cry about? Even if you don't have a green thumb, even if you're not sure about the weather or the soil conditions, seeds are full of hope, signs of possibility.

Throughout Advent, we hear the prophets proclaim hope to the people. But at the root of this hope is God's hard cure: the removal of all our attempts to save ourselves. We can't shore up our own hope; we have to wait on God. This is what makes faith such a powerful and costly gift. By trusting in God, we live like the ancient Israelites, not seeing what we hope for—in fact, much of the time, seeing the opposite. We may know God's plan of peace, but that belief must play out in small, daily gestures and attitudes of relinquishment and trust. Each day we plant the precious seed of our lives, hopes, and work, seed that will flourish only in the sun and air of God's kingdom, with no guarantee of its earthly success or when we might taste its fruit.

"Unless a grain of wheat falls into the earth and dies, it remains just a single grain," Jesus said (John 12:24). And that is the sorrow of the sower. We steward our lives to become experts at letting them go freely, as if there may not be any return, with complete abandonment to the soil of God's grace.

Our lives are fragile. "All people are grass," as Isaiah puts it (40:6). Plans, dreams, and relationships fail. Work is not enough. And yet each quiet attempt at faithfulness in any of these areas, each courageous step of faith, is a seed planted in the field of the Lord. Though sown in weeping, "the word of our God will stand forever" (Isa 40:8). Take heart! There will be a harvest!

Prayer for the Week

Merciful God, who sent your messengers the prophets to preach repentance and prepare the way for our salvation: Give us grace to heed their warnings and forsake our sins, that we may greet with joy the coming of Jesus Christ our Redeemer; who lives and reigns with you and the Holy Spirit, one God, now and for ever. *Amen.*

Reflective Practice

Ask yourself this question today in a quiet moment of meditation: do I feel like my arms are full of joyful harvest, or am I sowing in tears? Or is it a combination of both? Where you are enjoying abundance, with whom can you share it? Where you are sowing without apparent reward, when can you take a moment of rest to let the Lord refresh you?

Notes

_____

_____

_____

_____

_____

_____

_____

_____

_____

TUESDAY

Children of the Day

(▶) Open Dwell and listen to the following in the *Wonder* plan:
Psalm 126 | Isaiah 19:18-25 | 2 Peter 1:2-15

"Bible teaching about the Second Coming of Christ was thought of as 'doomsday' preaching. But not anymore. It is the only ray of hope that shines as an ever brightening beam in a darkening world."

-THE REVEREND BILLY GRAHAM

In Scripture, "on that day" refers to "the day of the Lord"—a time that Scripture also describes as "great and terrible" (Joel 2:31). Though this ultimately refers to Christ's Second Advent, "the day of the Lord" is any moment or era of time in which God arrives in person and acts in a decisive, salvific way. Every act of judgment and deliverance in the Old Testament was a dream of that day. The conception of Jesus in the womb of Mary was the first breath of dawn, the rising of the morning star of that day. With Jesus' birth, baptism, and ministry, God's light broke on the world. In his death, resurrection, and ascension, he broke the bonds that keep us from that light. We are now "children of the day" (1 Thess 5:5).

In ancient and contemporary liturgies, the Church refers to Christ as the one "who was, and is, and is to come." His day has dawned; his day is now; his day has yet to be. Each time it has come, "that day" has increased in scope and intensity. When Christ returns, it will break the bonds of time and finally, completely secure our *shalom*.

And yet, if we think we know what this means for us, Isaiah warns that there may be surprises. On "that day," Israel will see not just herself but her former enemies, the Egyptian slaveholders, becoming the Lord's own. We are reminded in this Advent reading that God's people, though first to see his salvation, have no ultimate upper hand in his favor and are not given one inch of space for pride.

St. Peter was the first to see salvation dawn on the Gentiles. He is the one who says to us today, as we wait for the coming of the Prince of Peace, not to forget that, though God's salvation is sure, it does not fit in a box. The day of the Lord is also the day of fear, partly because mercy is such a great shock to a world used to darkness.

Prayer for the Week

Merciful God, who sent your messengers the prophets to preach repentance and prepare the way for our salvation: Give us grace to heed their warnings and forsake our sins, that we may greet with joy the coming of Jesus Christ our Redeemer; who lives and reigns with you and the Holy Spirit, one God, now and for ever. *Amen.*

Reflective Practice

While it is more likely that we're in need of sleep than that we're getting too much of it, there is something powerful about praying at unusual times. If you're able, find a day this week in which you can either get up in the middle of the night or at sunrise and spend 20-30 minutes "keeping vigil" with the Lord. Try a simple spoken prayer, such as the Jesus Prayer: "Lord Jesus Christ, have mercy on me, a sinner." *(If you have a condition that makes sleep difficult for you, skip this practice and receive God's rest.)*

Notes

_____

_____

_____

_____

_____

_____

_____

WEDNESDAY

Restore Our Fortunes

▶ Open Dwell and listen to the following in the *Wonder* plan:
Psalm 126 | Isaiah 35:3-7 | Luke 7:18-30

"The Preparatory Prayer is to ask grace of God our Lord that all my intentions, actions and operations may be directed purely to the service and praise of his Divine Majesty. The second is to ask God our Lord for what I want and desire."

-St. Ignatius of Loyola

The reign of God is fulfilled in stages, often slowly and secretly, like planted seed. And yet, God's people have always prayed to see sudden and dramatic change in their world. Is this an appropriate prayer? Or one that lacks patience or faith?

To ask for God to come, come *now*, and bring his deliverance fully to bear on our lives can actually be an act of profound faith. And Scripture gives us permission and authority—perhaps even injunction—to do so. "O God, make speed to save us. O Lord, make haste to help us" is a powerful line of Evening Prayer in the Book of Common Prayer, from Psalm 70:1. In Psalm 126, we outright ask God to *"restore our fortunes . . .* like the watercourses in the Negev" (v 4). The watercourses of the Negev were dry and barren most of the time. They were only "restored" after a rare, sudden, and violent rainstorm that caused damaging floods but afterward left fertile ground. Isaiah tells the people to brace themselves for this kind of sudden salvation: "Make firm the feeble knees. . . . Here is your God. He will come and save you" (35:3-4). Like Psalm 126, Isaiah uses the image of a torrent transforming a desert into a place where water is not only found but over-abundant: a "swamp," a marshland (v 7). It is a place and time of dramatic cleansing, provision, and miraculous healing (v 5-6).

Isaiah implies that it requires courage to ask for and receive the gift God wants to give: his presence among us. It takes faith to wait for God, but just as much faith to accept and desire him as the mighty, rushing fountainhead of blessing that he is. It's a bit of a paradox to ask for God to hurry and then to be patient. But it is simply a longing for God's kingdom and trust that it will come. It is the practice that makes God's people.

Prayer for the Week

Merciful God, who sent your messengers the prophets to preach repentance and prepare the way for our salvation: Give us grace to heed their warnings and forsake our sins, that we may greet with joy the coming of Jesus Christ our Redeemer; who lives and reigns with you and the Holy Spirit, one God, now and for ever. *Amen.*

Reflective Practice

Have you ever asked God for something big, something that could not happen without his intervention? Today, come "boldly before the throne of grace" to ask of God the impossible and then ask for the grace to receive what he sends.

Notes

_____

_____

_____

_____

_____

_____

_____

_____

_____

THURSDAY

Learning to Grieve

▶ Open Dwell and listen to the following in the *Wonder* plan:
Isaiah 12:2-6 | Amos 6:1-8 | 2 Corinthians 8:1-15

"Pride makes us forget our sins, for the remembrance of them leads to humility."

-St. John Climacus

Advent is an invitation to step into the messiness of the world around us and the chaos within. This is a difficult invitation to accept, as it is far easier to distract and entertain in an attempt to avoid the difficult work of true transformation. However, conformity to the likeness of Christ, as his Incarnation makes abundantly clear, requires a willingness to set comfort aside in the name of self-giving, sacrificial love.

Put another way, difficult as it surely is to hear, Advent is an invitation to grieve.

Grief is an essential part of a life of true repentance. In Amos 6, the prophet's fundamental critique of the elite is their failure to grieve over the misery and suffering of their neighbors (Amos 6:6). Instead of using their means to care for the poor and needy, they use their resources to isolate themselves, keeping their senses constantly stimulated so as to not be reminded of the needs that surround them.

Though in many ways our world and Amos's couldn't be more different, the ways in which we as humans escape into ourselves are remarkably universal. Like Amos's list in verses 4-6, we too insulate ourselves from grief by sleeping, lounging on the couch, eating great food, drinking wine, splurging on beauty products, and playing music.

Our desire for comfort is deeper than we dare admit. It leads us to justify countless decisions and silence our hearts and lives to the cries of the poor and needy, not to mention our own heart's longing to be set free, which is the cry we most consistently and frequently ignore. Yet, into our comfortable isolation, each year the vulnerability of the manger calls to us, inviting us out of ourselves and into the world, learning to grieve with those who grieve and mourn with those who mourn (Rom 12:15).

Prayer for the Week

Merciful God, who sent your messengers the prophets to preach repentance and prepare the way for our salvation: Give us grace to heed their warnings and forsake our sins, that we may greet with joy the coming of Jesus Christ our Redeemer; who lives and reigns with you and the Holy Spirit, one God, now and for ever. *Amen.*

Reflective Practice

What creature comforts do you most firmly cling to? How do these comforts close you off from genuine and sacrificial love for your neighbor?

Notes

FRIDAY

Divine Blessing

(▶) Open Dwell and listen to the following in the *Wonder* plan:
Isaiah 12:2-6 | Amos 8:4-12 | 2 Corinthians 9:1-15

"Do not rely on your own ability, and God will come to your aid."

-ABBA AMMONAS

In a rich and affluent Western world, it is easy to read St. Paul's words in 2 Corinthians through a materialistic lens: "And God is able to provide you with every blessing in abundance, so that by always having enough of everything, you may share abundantly in every good work" (2 Cor 9:8). On the one hand, we can read these words as an affirmation of an already lavish lifestyle, taking it as a sure sign of God's blessing and favor upon our lives. On the other hand, for those living on the edge, hanging on by a thread and dreaming of financial freedom and security, these words from Paul are words of hope. They long for this to be a sign that their fortunes will soon change. Could it be, however, that both expectations miss the point entirely?

Here's a question to consider: are the blessings we long to receive from God blessings that only he can give? Rephrased slightly, are *God's* blessings the greatest desire of our lives? For those with enough education and influence, a life of material blessing and wealth can be acquired, seemingly without any divine intervention or assistance. Perhaps, then, there is a disconnect between our default definition of "blessing" and the abundance that God, in fact, wants to lavish upon us?

At the heart of the season of Advent lies a foundational question: what kind of lives are we meant to live as we anticipate the Lord's return, his *Second* Advent? According to Paul, we are meant to spend our days "sharing abundantly in every good work." We join in the work of the eternal kingdom *in the present*. We live lives that point to the humility and selfless love of our Lord and King. We learn daily to die to ourselves so that we may learn to truly live. *This* is a divine gift, a holy blessing that can only come from God's gracious hand.

Prayer for the Week

Merciful God, who sent your messengers the prophets to preach repentance and prepare the way for our salvation: Give us grace to heed their warnings and forsake our sins, that we may greet with joy the coming of Jesus Christ our Redeemer; who lives and reigns with you and the Holy Spirit, one God, now and for ever. *Amen.*

Reflective Practice

Take time to reflect on your definition of a "blessed life." How closely does it align with the biblical vision of true blessing and abundance?

Notes

SATURDAY

The Awe of Advent

(▶) Open Dwell and listen to the following in the *Wonder* plan:
Isaiah 12:2-6 | Amos 9:8-15 | Luke 1:57-66

*"The soul's desire is satisfied by the very fact that it remains insatiable.
For truly seeing God consists in never being satiated with desiring Him."*

-St. Gregory of Nyssa

You cannot worship God unless you are in awe of God. It is possible to respect him, honor him, and even follow him, yet fail to truly worship him. Advent, therefore, is an invitation for us to worship God as we are overcome with awe at the birth of Christ.

In this season, it is easy to focus on the *humanity* of Jesus, and rightly so. In Christ, the uncreated Word of God enters into his own creation as a creature. He is God with us so that we might be with him. Yes, Jesus is the babe in the manger, meek and mild, yet have centuries of sentimentality blinded us to what the Wise Men saw so clearly? This babe is the singular source of unceasing wonder and awe, the fullness of God contained within a living, breathing child.

Awe requires attentiveness. Our Lord does not force himself upon his creation, but enters in love and invites a response. God is our salvation, yet a response to this salvation is required. Like Isaiah, we must choose to trust and not be afraid (Isa 12:2). In Christ, the well of salvation is filled with living water, yet will we approach and drink with joy (Isa 12:3)?

Our awe of God deepens and grows as we meditate upon his faithfulness and reorient our lives to his promise. We long to welcome our Lord on Christmas Day with hearts made ready and overflowing with worship, wonder, and awe. Let us begin that work today, for truly, "great in your midst is the Holy One of Israel" (Isa 12:6).

Prayer for the Week

Merciful God, who sent your messengers the prophets to preach repentance and prepare the way for our salvation: Give us grace to heed their warnings and forsake our sins, that we may greet with joy the coming of Jesus Christ our Redeemer; who lives and reigns with you and the Holy Spirit, one God, now and for ever. *Amen.*

Reflective Practice

While God alone brings the rain, we must learn to cultivate and tend to the soil of our lives. Do you have a rhythm of regular meditation on Scripture, deepening and expanding your worship and wonder of our Lord?

Notes

THIRD WEEK *of* ADVENT

SUNDAY

In Our Midst

(▶) Open Dwell and listen to the following in the *Wonder* plan:
Zephaniah 3:14-20 | Isaiah 12:2-6 | Philippians 4:4-7 | Luke 3:7-18

"There is no space where God is not; space does not exist apart from Him. He is in heaven, in hell, beyond the seas; dwelling in all things and enveloping all."

-St. Hilary of Poitiers

Throughout the Bible, joy for the people of God is rooted not in the absence of conflict but in the nearness of God.

In Zephaniah 3:17, God is in their midst as "a warrior who gives victory." A warrior is only needed when faced with the reality of a real and present danger. Though the language of war and violence has fallen out of favor in our modern day, this imagery rightly understood brings with it profound comfort and, yes, joy.

Joy in a warrior God is entirely dependent upon your place within the story.

For those who oppose the ways of God, calling evil good and good evil (Isa 5:20), God in their midst is a source of conflict, a warrior to be resisted and opposed at every turn. Yet for the oppressed and enslaved, whose dignity as an image bearer of God has been exploited and shamefully abused, the presence of this same warrior is welcomed as liberation and salvation.

Could it be, if and when we struggle with Old Testament images of God, it has more to do with our blindness to our true desperation than it does with the goodness and character of God? For the truly oppressed, the deepest cry of their hearts is for a victorious warrior to come and fight on their behalf, to give victory over the enemies that dominate their daily lives.

In this third week of Advent, we are invited to enter into the joy of the nearness of God, "for great in your midst is the Holy One of Israel" (Isa 12:6). For us, this joy is rooted in God's simultaneous love for his children *and* his steadfast opposition to everything that seeks our harm or destruction. To do otherwise would be a failure to love. And so, as we draw nearer to Christmas Day, let us rejoice today with St. Paul, for truly "the Lord is near" (Phil 4:5).

Prayer for the Week

Stir up your power, O Lord, and with great might come among us; and, because we are sorely hindered by our sins, let your bountiful grace and mercy speedily help and deliver us; through Jesus Christ our Lord, to whom, with you and the Holy Spirit, be honor and glory, now and for ever. *Amen.*

Reflective Practice

What is the greatest threat to your joy? Reflect on the ways the nearness of God is for your good and your joy, coming as a strong warrior to set you free from all that oppresses and entangles.

Notes

_____

_____

_____

_____

_____

_____

_____

_____

_____

MONDAY

Remember Your Leaders

▶ Open Dwell and listen to the following in the *Wonder* plan:
Isaiah 11:1-9 | Numbers 16:1-19 | Hebrews 13:7-17

"Though the Christian may pray alone, he has the choir of the saints with him."

-St. Clement of Alexandria

When Jesus Christ entered the world, he did not come as an isolated individual but was born into a family. This family connection had an immediate expression through his mother Mary and adoptive father Joseph, yet also extended through them into the past. He received Israel's history as his own and likewise took their collective hopes and dreams upon himself as he fulfilled the mission given to him by the Father.

In a similar way, today we remember that our own living connection to Christ is not isolated from others but is nurtured and sustained within the community of faith.

We receive the words of Hebrews with grateful hearts as we remember the leaders who spoke God's word to us (Heb 13:7). Though God can speak directly to his children, such as in St. Paul's Damascus Road experience, he most often draws us to himself *through others*. And even in Paul's case, the Lord's direct word still led him to immediately seek out the community of faithful believers (Acts 9:6).

Remembering our leaders is both an act of gratitude for the past *and* inspiration for the present.

To be led to Christ is not simply to be shown a set of beliefs or historical positions but is fundamentally an invitation into a way of life. Leaders, at their best, bring us to the water *and* teach us how to drink. Hebrews encourages us to diligently observe and imitate their way of life. This is true of the immediate mentors and heroes in our lives, yet equally true of the great saints that have gone before. The life of God in the soul of the believer is a source of hope and inspiration in all times and all places, for as we are reminded today, "Jesus Christ is the same yesterday and today and forever" (Heb 13:8).

Prayer for the Week

Stir up your power, O Lord, and with great might come among us; and, because we are sorely hindered by our sins, let your bountiful grace and mercy speedily help and deliver us; through Jesus Christ our Lord, to whom, with you and the Holy Spirit, be honor and glory, now and for ever. *Amen.*

Reflective Practice

Who has most inspired and shaped your life with Christ? Take time today to give thanks for them in prayer, and if possible, reach out to them to express gratitude for their investment in your faith journey.

Notes

TUESDAY

Home Renovation

(▶) Open Dwell and listen to the following in the *Wonder* plan:
Isaiah 11:1-9 | Numbers 16:20-35 | Acts 28:23-31

"Jesus Christ, in His infinite love, has become what we are, in order that He may make us entirely what He is."

-St. Irenaeus of Lyons

During Advent, it is common to emphasize the *nearness* of God. In Jesus, God draws near to us. Yet closely related to this beautiful truth is the reality of God's *abiding* presence. As some translations put it, the Word became flesh and *made his home with us* (John 1:14).

Homemaking is, by definition, an act of settling that invites ongoing investment. When you are renting a home, for the most part you leave it as you found it, careful to not damage the flooring or scuff the paint. You are near, and even present, yet it isn't truly *home*. However, when you *own* a home, you take the lead on what it is and what it will become! In a sense, nothing is off-limits, with fresh paint often leading to renovated rooms and reimagined floor plans.

When Christ makes his home with us, he is refusing to simply enter and leave it as he found it. As the Lord of all creation, it is and has always been his home to renovate and restore as he sees fit. In his Incarnation, he reveals this eternal truth to us in love. Christ sees his creation suffering under the sickness of sin. He is deeply aware of the countless ways our brokenness leaves us tattered and torn. Yet, he is not indifferent to our pain, drawing near to renovate *from within* as owner and resident.

In doing so, Jesus reveals a way of living that we are meant to emulate: healing comes as we are present to others in the name of the Lord. This is seen today in Acts 28, as St. Paul makes his home in Rome for two years, giving the local community the *gift of presence* (Acts 28:30). He proclaimed the kingdom of God as one who was known, loved, and trusted.

Where and with whom do we make our home? In an ever-changing and transient society, what might it look like for us to stick around and remain present to others in the name of the Lord? As Christ makes his home with us, we must learn to go and do the same, dwelling with him and staying present to those he loves, for this is the way of true renovation.

Prayer for the Week

Stir up your power, O Lord, and with great might come among us; and, because we are sorely hindered by our sins, let your bountiful grace and mercy speedily help and deliver us; through Jesus Christ our Lord, to whom, with you and the Holy Spirit, be honor and glory, now and for ever. *Amen.*

Reflective Practice

Where, or with whom, do you feel most at home? How can Christ's unwavering commitment to make his home with us shape and impact your own sense of belonging and welcome into the family of God?

Notes

WEDNESDAY

Shoots From a Stump

(▶) Open Dwell and listen to the following in the *Wonder* plan:
Isaiah 11:1-9 | Micah 4:8-13 | Luke 7:31-35

"Believe me, if you knew Who is with you, you would not fear anything the world has to offer."

-St. Macarius The Great

In order to faithfully read and appreciate the Old Testament, it is profoundly helpful to view Israel through a familial lens.

Israel was a family that had within its history moments of profound hope and joy as they walked in the ways of the Lord, yet at the same time endured entire generations of shame and scandal. As we reflect upon this family's story in Advent, we come upon a particularly bleak moment in their history, with many wondering how any of the promises of old could be kept. Surely the Israelites' story had reached a dead end of their own making?

Isaiah had a unique ability to identify the severity of a problem while still holding out an unwavering hope for the future.

Instead of a mature tree with centuries of growth and vitality, Isaiah spoke of Israel as a stump. Typically, a stump is the end of the road for a tree, a remnant and shadow of its former self left simply to rot and decay. Yet, without denying the tragedy that is a tree reduced to a stump, the Lord, through Isaiah, spoke words of unimaginable hope: "A shoot shall come out from the stump of Jesse, and a branch shall grow out of his roots" (Isa 11:1).

In thinking of your own story, you may resonate with this image of a stump.

Whether rooted in your immediate circumstances or the wider family story to which you belong, it may be that this Advent season reaches you in a particularly painful and disorienting time. As with Isaiah, acknowledging this reality is the first step of living by truth and not lies. Yet do not miss the second step and even greater truth! Our Lord is at work, even now, bringing beauty out of ashes and life out of death, with shoots of hope springing forth from the stumps of our broken stories.

Prayer for the Week

Stir up your power, O Lord, and with great might come among us; and, because we are sorely hindered by our sins, let your bountiful grace and mercy speedily help and deliver us; through Jesus Christ our Lord, to whom, with you and the Holy Spirit, be honor and glory, now and for ever. *Amen.*

Reflective Practice

Are there parts of your life that, instead of growing into a flourishing tree, have been reduced to a stump? Believing that God tells good stories, what shoots of new life might be springing forth from the stumps of your life, bringing with them the healing and restoration that only he can give?

Notes

_____

_____

_____

_____

_____

_____

_____

_____

_____

THURSDAY

Restore Us, O Lord

▶ Open Dwell and listen to the following in the *Wonder* plan:
Psalm 80:1-7 | Jeremiah 31:31-34 | Hebrews 10:10-18

"God requires not the doing of the commandments for their own sake, but the correction of the soul, for whose sake He established the commandments."

-ST. ISAAC THE SYRIAN

"Restore us, O Lord!" We will hear this refrain this week in Psalm 80. This is what God's people cry when their enemies have overtaken them, when natural disaster strikes, or when their lives are devastated or destroyed. God's people are even gutsy enough to cry for restoration when they know the trouble they're in is a result of their own waywardness!

Even though going astray like sheep and crying for the shepherd's rescue is a pattern as old as time and a stage for the Good Shepherd's faithfulness, it can become a rut, and we can forget that there's more God has for us. One of the tensions of Advent is between our neediness, weakness, and sin and John the Baptist's cry to "prepare the way of the Lord." We are broken and confused creatures, and yet we are called to holiness.

"Restore us!" will be our cry until Christ returns, but the way God restores us has changed since the psalmist's time. The prophet Jeremiah reminds us that though God's people are constantly breaking the old covenant, God is already at work to write a new one on their hearts. According to this new way, God's people are not doomed to the same failure-rescue-failure routine, but God will write his law inside them, transforming their inmost selves, as well as guiding and guarding their outward actions.

Those who belong to God always remain his children, his sheep. As long as we are creatures (which we will always be), we will be limited, small, and have needs. That's part of what it means to be human. But the new covenant arriving in Christ lets us grow up to be spiritually mature, adult children in God's household. The "full stature of Christ" (Eph 4:13) is the promise before us—not only rescue and restoration. Or perhaps it's better to say this is the restoration God intended for us all along but was waiting to reveal.

Prayer for the Week

Stir up your power, O Lord, and with great might come among us; and, because we are sorely hindered by our sins, let your bountiful grace and mercy speedily help and deliver us; through Jesus Christ our Lord, to whom, with you and the Holy Spirit, be honor and glory, now and for ever. *Amen.*

Reflective Practice

List 10-20 characteristics of a mature person (e.g., honesty, forbearance, patience, good boundaries, genuine affection, etc.). In your prayer time today, consider going through each of these characteristics and making each one a prayer for yourself, your family, your workplace, your church, or your nation. Begin with "Restore us, O Lord," and then name the Christlike quality, asking that it be planted and nourished in yourself and others.

Notes

_____

_____

_____

_____

_____

_____

_____

FRIDAY

Sing and Shout

(▶) Open Dwell and listen to the following in the *Wonder* plan:
Psalm 80:1-7 | Isaiah 42: 10-18 | Hebrews 10:32-29

"If we wish to serve God and love our neighbor well, we must manifest our joy in the service we render to Him and them. Let us open wide our hearts. It is joy which invites us. Press forward and fear nothing."

-St. Katharine Drexel

Maybe going to a few parties during Advent is not such a bad idea after all. But if we're going to stick with the themes of Advent, we'd need to trade hors d'oeuvres and polite conversation for dancing, singing, and shouting. We're celebrating with a serious purpose. Today in Isaiah, we hear a call to sing and shout because God is fulfilling a promise to come to his people, to finally come "against his foes" (Isa 42:11-13).

The "foes" the Lord comes against are those who prop up the power of "carved images" (Isa 42:17)—gods of pretension and empty glamor. In biblical times, as well as our own, all false gods represented some form of violence, greed, or coercion. God comes to save us from these powers from without and from within.

Hebrews invites us even more deeply into this serious joy. The writer tells us that once we are "enlightened," filled with God's light and walking with him in the light, the false gods will start fighting back. But God will give us the power to participate with him in loving transformation. In the "sufferings" and loss (Isa 10:32-34) that are inspired by violence, greed, and coercion, God's people are given his light and joy to share with their neighbors through a witness of endurance, compassion, and non-violence. We may even see a holy sense of humor at play as God's people see through the pretensions of earthly power: even when their property is taken or destroyed, they are still impossibly cheerful because they know they have "something better" (v 34).

Today we see that the waiting and promises of Advent include God's desire, not only to save us, not only to mature us, but to bring us into his own work of witness. Our God-given graciousness has the power to lead others to salvation. And that is a reason to party.

Prayer for the Week

Stir up your power, O Lord, and with great might come among us; and, because we are sorely hindered by our sins, let your bountiful grace and mercy speedily help and deliver us; through Jesus Christ our Lord, to whom, with you and the Holy Spirit, be honor and glory, now and for ever. *Amen.*

Reflective Practice

In a moment of prayer today, ask the Lord how you might share your home, possessions, or other resources this Advent or Christmas season. Then spend a few moments in silence, writing down any ideas that may come. Is there something you can give away? Is there a party you'd like to host? Could you commit to only watching television or movies in community, rather than alone? As you feel led, make a plan to do one of the things that come to mind.

Notes

_____

_____

_____

_____

_____

_____

_____

_____

SATURDAY

The Love of a Mother

▶ Open Dwell and listen to the following in the *Wonder* plan:
Psalm 80:1-7 | Isaiah 66:7-11 | Luke 13:31-35

"Mary, mother of Jesus, please be a mother to me now."

-St. Theresa of Calcutta (Mother Theresa)

In Advent, Jesus is still an unborn infant, but in today's passage from Luke 13, he compares himself to a mother, and God's people are his babies. This must have sounded shocking to his hearers. And yet, it makes sense, especially when we consider his own mother.

We can rightly imagine that Mary was an excellent mother. We can rightly imagine that Jesus was blessed by her and experienced the grace of the Father through her care, discipline, example, and love. When Jesus gives us this tender and moving image of himself as a mother hen gathering a flock of tiny, helpless chicks under his wings, we may rightly imagine he thought of his mother, and perhaps his own childhood, even as he thought of Israel's history.

Jesus gives us much more in this image than we can take in on first contemplation. But steeping in the promises of Advent—of our victorious, bright-faced, swift-arriving Savior—we would miss out if we did not also contemplate the tenderness and vulnerability of the Incarnation. In an act of sheer loving-kindness, God the Son enters the human experience. In many ways, a human baby is as helpless as a baby chick. God the Son would now need help, protection, feeding, and love.

And yet, through God's providence and Mary and Joseph's care, and perhaps by the love and care of many others, Jesus will grow up to identify Mary's motherly love and vocation with his own. As he realizes his identity and the Father's will for his life, Jesus will turn his own mother-like love toward his people. We can hear in this passage his yearning—God's own yearning—to help us, protect us, feed us, and love us, even at our most lost, wayward, helpless, vulnerable, and confused.

As we anticipate being with Mary in the stable as she looks upon the newborn Jesus for the first time, let us also anticipate Jesus' gaze back toward us, full of every spark of the jealous love of Israel's strong, delivering God and every bit of Mary's tenderness.

Prayer for the Week

Stir up your power, O Lord, and with great might come among us; and, because we are sorely hindered by our sins, let your bountiful grace and mercy speedily help and deliver us; through Jesus Christ our Lord, to whom, with you and the Holy Spirit, be honor and glory, now and for ever. *Amen.*

Reflective Practice

In Greek, Jesus' mother is known as the Theotokos, the "God-bearer." She bore Jesus and bore God's presence and grace in a special way. What more can we learn about Jesus and his love by considering Mary? Find an image or icon of Mary that speaks to your heart, and spend 15-20 minutes in quiet prayer before the Lord, contemplating this extraordinary woman. Ask Jesus to show you something of his own heart in hers.

Notes

FOURTH WEEK *of* ADVENT

SUNDAY

Small and Humble

▶ Open Dwell and listen to the following in the *Wonder* plan:
Micah 5:2-5 | Psalm 80:1-7 | Hebrews 10:5-10 | Luke 1:39-55

"When anyone is disturbed or saddened under the pretext of a good and soul-profiting matter, and is angered against his neighbor, it is evident that this is not according to God: for everything that is of God is peaceful and useful and leads a man to humility."

-St. Barsanuphius The Great

How do we know what God is really like?

We know God is love (at least, we've been told). And yet, as fallen humans—even as people who believe in God—it is all too easy to get tangled up in mistaken notions about him, whether from incomplete or inaccurate teaching and preaching or from difficult and broken relationships with parents, pastors, other authority figures, or for many other reasons. We can even have wrong *ideas* about the accurate *words* we associate with God, such as "holy" or "jealous" or "perfect." Anything that invites discouragement or distance rather than desire and joy in our relationship with God can often be traced back to this kind of misunderstanding.

As with God's people long ago, there are many false "gods" around us. We, too, need the Lord to remind us of who he is and make our imaginations healthy so we can know him better, more deeply, and more freely.

Today, here is a simple yet profound reminder from Micah of God's character and how we will recognize it in the Messiah. We hear that God will intentionally select what is little to make it great (5:2). A characteristic of God's love is that it gravitates to what is small and humble. As we learn more about God's love this week, let's use Micah 5:2-5 as a guide. If we cannot picture a God whose eye is on "one of the little clans of Judah," then we have the wrong god. By choosing Judah to be his own birthplace, God honors what no one else is honoring because God is someone who honors what humans often miss. In all his might, he is *more* gentle, *more* sensitive, *more* kind than we can imagine. He makes the small great, then makes his grandest and humblest entrances there.

Prayer for the Week

Purify our conscience, Almighty God, by your daily visitation, that your Son Jesus Christ, at his coming, may find in us a mansion prepared for himself; who lives and reigns with you, in the unity of the Holy Spirit, one God, now and for ever. *Amen.*

Reflective Practice

What areas of your life seem "small"? What people or circumstances stand out to you that others seem to overlook? Bring these to God in prayer. Name each person or circumstance before him. Ask God to honor each one of them through the presence of Christ. If you get a sense of how the Lord would like to show his love, either write it down to continue holding it in prayer this week or ask God how he might like you to participate.

Notes

_____

_____

_____

_____

_____

_____

_____

_____

_____

MONDAY

Longing for Home

▶ Open Dwell and listen to the following in the *Wonder* plan:
Psalm 113 | Genesis 25:19-28 | Colossians 1:15-20

"Brothers and Sisters! The all-merciful God desires happiness for us both in this life and in the life to come. Let us hasten, and the Church will lift the weight of our burdens, give us boldness before God, and fill our hearts with happiness and blessedness."

-St. Nectarius of Aegina

Today we hear of childless women miraculously conceiving, the barren becoming fruitful. With so many hopes in our hearts unfulfilled—for some of us, childless homes that have longed to welcome a child—how do we hear this message as a hopeful sign of God's love?

In our passage from Colossians, we also hear one of the most beautiful hymns about Christ ever written. This hymn shows us the cosmic sweep of Christ's ministry, from before creation to the end of the age. In Christ himself, in his own person, the mystery of all our deepest—often painful—longings and their fulfillment are revealed. We long to be healed, fruitful, thriving, happy, peaceful, hopeful, and joyful precisely because we were made in and through the very Son of God, the Father's Beloved. To put the hymn from Colossians a little differently, he is where we are from, where we belong, and where we are going. All of our longings to make a home, complete a home, share a home, or return home are rooted in our Home, Jesus.

God's love is the birthplace of all our truest longings. For those of us who receive some satisfaction of those longings in this life, let us thank the giver of good gifts. But all satisfactions and answered prayers are signs and tastes of the gift God specially prepares for each of us: peace, wholeness, and "the fullness of God" himself (Col 1:19). This may not make the pain of prayer and waiting any easier, but it does tell us about the one who loves us and that he is preparing more than just enough for us—he is preparing full satisfaction. In fact, amazingly, he is preparing this satisfaction for every creature ("all things"). If even every sparrow has God's attention, as Jesus puts it, how much more those of us with the longing, desiring human nature he gladly shares?

Prayer for the Week

Purify our conscience, Almighty God, by your daily visitation, that your Son Jesus Christ, at his coming, may find in us a mansion prepared for himself; who lives and reigns with you, in the unity of the Holy Spirit, one God, now and for ever. *Amen.*

Reflective Practice

Take up to 30 minutes to notice all the creatures around you other than humans. Every time you see one—a squirrel, a cat, a blue jay, a beetle—consider the ways God provides for this creature, both by his grace and with their participation. How does he "home" them? At the end of this exercise, or at the end of the day, consider how God is making a home for you in this season. How might he be calling you more deeply to make your home in him, in your church, or in your community?

Notes

_____

_____

_____

_____

_____

_____

_____

TUESDAY

Faithful Waiting

▶ Open Dwell and listen to the following in the *Wonder* plan:
Psalm 113 | Genesis 30:1-24 | Romans 8:18-30

"Never despair of the mercy of God."

-ST. ISIDORE OF SEVILLE

"I consider that the sufferings of this present time are not worth comparing with the glory about to be revealed to us" (Rom 8:18). What if St. Paul could have spoken this to Rachel and Leah, and what if they could have believed it? Would their story still have been as full of drama as a reality TV show? They knew that God had promised Abraham, Sarah, Isaac, and Jacob that he would make a great nation of their family, a blessing to the whole earth. Even from their position, without knowing about Jesus, could they have put down their fear?

Perhaps that's easy to say. The promises of Advent are rich, precious, and true. But our hope, as St. Paul reminds us, lies in that which is not fully seen. That doesn't mean our hope is in the purely "spiritual" realm, apart from what we can ever see or touch—in fact, quite the opposite. Our ultimate hope is for what St. Paul elsewhere calls "the redemption of our bodies" (Rom 8:23). We're waiting for our very physical existence with all its desires, pleasures, complexities, and limits to be justified, healed, and revealed in a new way. How will it be done? We don't know exactly. When? Anyone's guess. And so, like Rachel and Leah, we wait. And try to be faithful. And it's one of the hardest things to do.

To Rachel and Leah's great credit (among other honors we give them), they knew God's promises were both personal and concrete. But expectations—even expectations of God—without encouragement and hope easily turn to disappointment, anger, envy, and fear.

The Lord is trustworthy. He will show up. But how? And when? Waiting and wading through the concrete details is hard. But the greatest evidence we have of his trustworthiness is the Incarnation itself. He said he would never leave us or forsake us. Can we dare to exercise that muscle of hope today?

Prayer for the Week

Purify our conscience, Almighty God, by your daily visitation, that your Son Jesus Christ, at his coming, may find in us a mansion prepared for himself; who lives and reigns with you, in the unity of the Holy Spirit, one God, now and for ever. *Amen.*

Reflective Practice

In a time of waiting, it can help to be open with the Lord and not hide our feelings. Where has your muscle of hope grown weak? Consider areas in your life where your hope has been disappointed or put on hold. It might help to journal or speak to God about them. It may also help to simply hold them silently in your mind during a time of prayer today, asking your heavenly Father to show you how he is providing for you.

Notes

_____

_____

_____

_____

_____

_____

_____

_____

_____

WEDNESDAY

Take Heart

(▶) Open Dwell and listen to the following in the *Wonder* plan:
Psalm 113 | Isaiah 42:14-21 | Luke 1:5-25

"The world was made partly that there may be prayer; partly that our prayers might be answered."

-C.S. LEWIS

Today's story in Luke is a perfect appetizer preparing us for what will come next. We see once again, but in an especially concentrated way, the character of the God who is about to come through wonderfully for his people. We see a God who:

Listens. Temple worship continues, the law is read, the people gather, priests offer incense—and God attends to the faithfulness he finds. Both in religion *and* relationship, God sees our attempts to please him. Though Elizabeth and Zechariah's lives weren't all they wanted them to be, and they surely weren't perfect people, God was happy with them. God was also listening to their prayers. How amazing would it be to hear, as Zechariah did after years of asking, "God has been listening to you"?

Sees. God is not looking at appearances but at the heart. When he chooses parents for his prophet, he chooses people willing to love and serve, whose fulfilled longing will bring joy to the whole community. That they are not at the "right" stage of life, that this seems impossible or even undignified at their age, makes no difference to God.

Acts. Every act of God is an act of truth-telling and love. And though he's full of rest, this is not a God who sits with hands folded. We get a peek behind the curtain and hear that he is on the job, judging right and wrong, considering every angle, choosing wisely, showing mercy, and providing abundantly.

We can take heart. If there seem to be pauses between God's acts, maybe they are like rests in music and not simply God losing the plot or failing to pay attention. God is *attentive*. Maybe Zechariah must be silent himself for a while to understand this. An ancient prayer called the *Te Deum* says simply and beautifully: "In you, Lord, is our hope. And we shall never hope in vain." It is a prayer of trust but also a song of praise. Like Elizabeth's song, it will be a song of vindication for all who trust in him.

Prayer for the Week

Purify our conscience, Almighty God, by your daily visitation, that your Son Jesus Christ, at his coming, may find in us a mansion prepared for himself; who lives and reigns with you, in the unity of the Holy Spirit, one God, now and for ever. *Amen.*

Reflective Practice

Spend at least 5 minutes (but as long as you wish) in silent prayer before God. Simply let yourself rest in his presence, with no agenda. Close your prayer time by slowly saying the last few lines of the *Te Deum*:

Have mercy on us, Lord, have mercy.

Lord, show us your love and mercy;

For we put our trust in you.

In you, Lord, is our hope:

And we shall never hope in vain.

Notes

_____

_____

_____

_____

DAYS *around*

CHRISTMAS

DECEMBER 22

The Highest Mountain

▶ Open Dwell and listen to the following in the *Wonder* plan:
Luke 1:46-55 | Micah 4:1-5 | Ephesians 2:11-22

"I think we must have great modesty and sobriety about ourselves, even if someone should think they are firmly fixed by the progress they have already made in establishing themselves in good deeds."

-St. Cyril of Alexandria

In the humble descent of our Lord Jesus, the highest mountain is established for all eternity.

If you've ever ascended a mountain, you know it to be a breathtaking experience. While the base of the mountain may be teeming with a diversity of life, the higher you go, the more narrow and limited your reality becomes. The trees thin out, the air becomes colder, and foliage and animal life becomes scarce. Quickly, one's focus is set entirely upon the summit, with other distractions soon fading away.

However, upon reaching the summit, the world is returned to you, though now seen through an entirely different lens. From the summit, the whole of existence is transformed, illumined in a new and exhilarating light. The individual pieces and experiences receive the gift of perspective, finding their place in the whole.

Jesus Christ is "the highest of the mountains" (Mic 4:1), to which the nations stream and from which we see the world as it is meant to be seen.

As Christmas draws near, we are invited to join our hearts with these words from Micah: "Come, let us go up to the mountain of the Lord, to the house of the God of Jacob; that he may teach us his ways and that we may walk in his paths" (Mic 4:2).

Jesus is both our destination and our journey, the mountain and the path. And so, let us look to Christ as the summit and aim of life, learning that our journey of *ascent* begins and is sustained only as we *descend*. Humility is the way to greatness, simplicity the path to true riches, and death the way that leads to life.

Prayer for the Week

Purify our conscience, Almighty God, by your daily visitation, that your Son Jesus Christ, at his coming, may find in us a mansion prepared for himself; who lives and reigns with you, in the unity of the Holy Spirit, one God, now and for ever. *Amen.*

Reflective Practice

As Christmas Day draws near, take time today to reflect upon the humility of our Lord, believing this to be the lens through which we learn to see the world as our Lord sees it.

Notes

DECEMBER 23

Shared Joy

▶ Open Dwell and listen to the following in the *Wonder* plan:
Luke 1:46-55 | Micah 4:6-8 | 2 Peter 1:16-21

"God does not open His Hand because we have closed up our hearts towards our brothers and sisters."

-St. Basil The Great

When we think of the Virgin Mary in and around the Christmas season, her words to the angel Gabriel often come to mind: "Here am I, the servant of the Lord; let it be with me according to your word" (Luke 1:38). Similarly, we join our hearts to hers and in prayer say, "My soul magnifies the Lord, and my spirit rejoices in God my Savior" (Luke 1:46-47). And while we should continue to learn from Mary's meekness and humility, Luke 1 also reveals to us her zeal and great desire to share this news with others.

The joy and hope Mary received in the Annunciation is meant to be experienced by all. She knew this, that she played a role in a much bigger story, that this announcement was the fulfillment of centuries of prophetic messages and shared longings. And so, she "set out and went with haste" to greet her cousin Elizabeth, an act which led to Elizabeth's own direct encounter with the living God (Luke 1:39-45).

Mary is celebrated and blessed in all generations (Luke 1:48) for her faithful reception of Christ as he drew near. Yet we must not forget how she freely shared her joy with those around her. As we long to know and encounter God, to have the life of Christ born within us this Christmas season, can we also join with Mary in seeking to share his life with others?

Growth in Christ moves us from looking only to our own wants and desires into a deep longing to see our friends, family, neighbors, and even our enemies filled with the Holy Spirit, and to discover, in St. Peter's words, the lamp that shines in a dark place (2 Pet 1:19).

Prayer for the Week

Purify our conscience, Almighty God, by your daily visitation, that your Son Jesus Christ, at his coming, may find in us a mansion prepared for himself; who lives and reigns with you, in the unity of the Holy Spirit, one God, now and for ever. *Amen.*

Reflective Practice

True joy cannot be contained nor kept in isolation! Explore ways to share the joy of this season today with your friends, family, and neighbors.

Notes

EVE *of* CHRISTMAS

DECEMBER 24

The Fire of God

(▶) Open Dwell and listen to the following in the *Wonder* plan:
Isaiah 62:6-12 | Psalm 97 | Titus 3:4-7 | Luke 2:1-20

"Blessed be the merciful One, who came and took a body which could suffer, that he might open the way into Paradise."

-ST. EPHREM THE SYRIAN

And the Lord comes. Here comes the King, the deliverer we've been waiting for, the promise, the sum of all answered prayer. When the psalmist says that "fire goes before him and consumes his adversaries on every side" (97:3), the *him* is this infant. And what fire goes before a baby?

The fire of God's Holy Spirit, who conceived him in Mary's womb.

The fire of God's judgment, which confounds earthly powers even as it submits to be registered by them.

The fire of God's cleansing, which made Zechariah mute and opened Joseph's eyes to the truth.

The fire of God's justice, which favored a small town and vindicated a young mother's patience.

The fire of the stars and angels, who proclaim his welcome.

The fire of God's joy, which greets the weary, third-shift shepherds.

The fire of God's eternal charity, which will always make a way and will always win.

We might recall God's provision as he led his people out of Egypt with a cloud by day and a fire by night. Even this was pointing to Jesus. The "cloud of unknowing," of waiting for God to show up and reveal himself, to deliver, to restore all the enemy had taken, lasted for thousands of years. Like a cloud, the law and the prophets covered, protected, and guided God's people through the long desert of history. Even Mary's miraculous pregnancy—one of God's most paradigm-shifting miracles—is like the cloud. "How can this be?" she asks, with thick mystery ahead of her, and she follows.

And now—suddenly!—God reveals himself. We're hardly ready! And yet, even as this fire given to guide us by night blazed brightly, its Lord was born quietly, gently, and nearly unnoticed. Like Mary, let us "ponder these things" in our hearts, still soaking in this mystery even as we bask in its light. Let us rest in preparation for tomorrow's feast of deliverance.

Prayer for Christmas Eve

O God, you have caused this holy night to shine with the brightness of the true Light: Grant that we, who have known the mystery of that Light on earth, may also enjoy him perfectly in heaven; where with you and the Holy Spirit he lives and reigns, one God, in glory everlasting. *Amen.*

Reflective Practice

Begin celebrating today, even in a small way. Enjoy a sample of a Christmas snack or drink. Open a present. As you do, create an intentional moment of giving thanks. If you're with family, housemates, or in a group, consider using this time to read aloud and reflect on the story from Luke. Help one another prepare your hearts to welcome tomorrow with joy.

Notes

_____

_____

_____

_____

_____

_____

DAY *of*

CHRISTMAS

DECEMBER 25

In the Beginning

Open Dwell and listen to the following in the *Wonder* plan:
Isaiah 52:7-10 | Psalm 98 | Hebrews 1:1-12 | John 1:1-14

"Today is born of the Virgin him who holds all creation in the hollow of His hand. He whose essence is untouchable is wrapped in swaddling clothes as a babe. The God who from of old established the heavens lies in a manger. He who showered the people with manna in the wilderness feeds on milk from the breasts."

-BYZANTINE HYMN OF THE NATIVITY

In the beginning. Three words begin both the book of Genesis and John's Gospel. This is neither a coincidence nor an accident! St. John, often referred to as "John the Theologian," is teaching us about the true nature of God in Christ Jesus. Just as the uncreated power of God hovered over the face of the deep, so too does that same creative power now dwell within the creation he spoke into being.

Familiarity, nostalgia, and sentimentally work together to numb us to the wonder of this truth. And yet, in his goodness and love, our Lord gives us the gift of seasons, rhythms of reflection and renewal. Every year on this day, we are invited to return to the same story, to reflect again and again upon the great mystery of the Word made flesh.

Though the story of Christmas is timeless, our *encounter* with Christ is as unique and varied as each of our individual stories. While you may have been filled with hope and optimism a year ago, today you may be overcome with grief and a sense of hopelessness. Hard work and determination slowly give way to apathy and disillusionment. Relational, professional, and emotional wounds leave you beaten and bruised.

Christmas Day marks the end of our Advent journey, yet it is as much a beginning as it is an end.

No matter what life may look like for you today, whether full of joy, sorrow, or an interwoven combination of both, this is a day of creation, of new life. It is the reminder that the Lord, who created at the very beginning, came into the world to continue that good creation and meets you today with the same invitation to find your place and new beginning within his story of creation.

Prayer for Christmas Day

Almighty God, you have given your only-begotten Son to take our nature upon him, and to be born this day of a pure virgin: Grant that we, who have been born again and made your children by adoption and grace, may daily be renewed by your Holy Spirit; through our Lord Jesus Christ, to whom with you and the same Spirit be honor and glory, now and for ever. *Amen.*

Reflective Practice

Having walked the road of Advent, enter now fully into the joy and delight of the Christmas season! Take the next twelve days to feast with your family and friends, letting your joy spill out into every area of your life, inviting others into the wonder of a God who draws near in love.

Notes

_____

_____

_____

_____

_____

_____

_____

Endnotes

Lectionary selections are reprinted from Revised Common Lectionary Daily Readings for Year B, copyright © 2005. Consultation on Common Texts, Augsburg Fortress Publishers. Reproduced by permission.

Scripture texts are from the New Revised Standard Version of the Bible, copyright © 1989 by the Division of Christian Education of the National Council of the Churches of Christ in the USA. All rights reserved. Used with permission.

Prayers are taken from *The Book Of Common Prayer and Administration of the Sacraments and Other Rites and Ceremonies of the Church: Together with the Psalter or Psalms of David According to the Use of the Episcopal Church*. New York: Seabury Press, 1979.

Made in the USA
Columbia, SC
02 November 2021